POEMS FROM HOME:
A CHILDREN'S ANTHOLOGY

If you look the right way, you can see that the whole world is a garden.

- Frances Hodgson Burnett

Our second edition of *Poems From Home: A Children's Anthology* has been no less fantastic to produce than the first.

To the children...
It really is a privilege to read your work, to see how you use language, and to appreciate the things you choose to write about. Sometimes your poems make me giggle, sometimes they really move me, but always they make me smile. You all have real talent and have produced some really lovely work and I hope that you are proud! Just imagine all the other children whose work is in this book, their families, and all the other people who will read the poems that YOU wrote!

To the adults...
Thank you again for your cooperation with the process, for sharing the project with others who would not otherwise have been able to take part, and for supporting and encouraging your children to join in!

To Matthew...
Thank you again for the time you put in with the illustrations, and for creating the cover artwork.

Jennifer Buckley, Editor

LIST OF AUTHORS

:LOVE & LIFE:

You are bound to have haters and lovers.
Haters say mean things like - "You will fail!", lovers say - "You will prevail!"

You have choices and choices are life.
If you say something nice, it could change someone's life.

When someone is sad give them a helping-hand,
when they are mad give them a comforting-hand!

When life asks you what you will do, just do what's true,
so that you can be the best to others too!

Haters will struggle, while you juggle.

When you live you love, and when you hate you are bait.

You always lose something but that's okay! So keep calm, it's okay.

You can always learn and improve, so win and don't lose.
Think positive and block out the haters, so you can be your best and thank yourself later.

- Kaisan

:TRAVELS:

The plane - like a bird in the sky or a train floating high.
The seats - like a big pillow or a bed that's little.
The food - a small buffet for you to eat away.
And the people - a blend of life with a bit of spice.

All of this, when traveling a world full of bliss.

There's always more to explore,
So don't stay at home all day,
Explore and have fun along the way.

- Kaisan

:HOPE & LIFE:

No matter how life goes, how much the rivers flow, you always know, that the places you go, always grow, a hope.

Deep inside them, lurks hope, And hope can do powerful things.

Hope can be your light in the dark, hope can make you feel bright and smart, when you're failing your test there's no solution better than this; hope.

And nobody is better than the rest, and nobody deserves to be called a pest.

So be good and not bad, for the bad make others sad and sometimes mad.

But the good should and would help.

The bad could've helped and would rather not have helped.

So don't let the bad turn you mad or sad, and definitely don't turn bad.

And always know that you are unique so do not weep.

- Laiq

:ART & HEART:

I grab a pencil or I use a stencil.
I can doodle or draw a poodle.
I can sketch and I can etch.
I know how to blend which is a godsend.
I can shade a blockade.
And all of this is art, which I throw like a dart.
And if you use your heart you too can produce art.

- Laiq

:WINTER IS…:

As quiet as trees,
Snowflakes are seen in the dark,
Frost is glitter in your head,
as kind as a snowman.
As slippery as ice.
As dark as the moon.
Dark as bats.
Light as the moon.
Light as life.
Light as friendship, reflecting off the sun.
Christmas is cake,
a snowman
and being happy.
Christmas is winter to me.

:HARRY THE DOG:

There once was a young dog named Harry.

Who happened to love eating chips.

He eats them all day.

In the most slow way.

But still finds time to sniff carrots!

- Fred, 9, Leicester

:VEGANISM IS…:

Veganism is a philosophy and a way of living.

Eat no meat.

Great meal substitutes

Are Tempeh, Seitan, Tofu, Black beans, lentils and Jackfruit.

No testing on animals for soap

Is ridiculed, mocked and dismissed.

Super vegan actors protesting for animal rights.

Meet Earth man, made from trees creates a refuge, he'd clear
plastic from the seas and stop animal slaughter!

- George, 10, Leicester

:SAVE OUR PLANET:

Save our planet or we'll be dead.

Don't run,

Don't hide !

Save our planet before it dies,

Give it love

Be nice

Be happy.

- George, 10, Leicester

:A PRISONER IN HAWAII:

A prisoner escaped,
broke the cell,
And changed its shape,

Never came back,
Flew to Hawaii,
Put on a magical hat,
To stay safe,
To enjoy the sun,
and the blue skies,
In a breathtaking place.

He found a base,
Guards stared,
Into his face,
And the answer was,
Let's race and chase.

- Amir Abdalla, 6, London.

:A HOME IN NATURE:

Nature is an infinite beauty,
Created by the All Mighty,
Gifted for all humanity,
To ponder in and glorify.

Trees are nature's roof,
Bushes are nature's walls,
Hills are nature's stairs,
Grass is nature's bed,
Sticks are nature's pipes.

Nature is an infinite beauty,
Created by the All Mighty,
Gifted for all humanity,
To ponder in and glorify.

- Omer Abdalla, 11, London

:BE KIND TO EVERYONE:

I love people big and small,
People who are tiny & people who are tall

I love people with a broken leg
I love people with a prosthetic leg

I love people who are deaf and blind
I love people who are disabled or kind

I love people big and small,
People who are tiny & people who are tall

I love people with different faiths
And people who are on wheelchairs as well

- Nour Ahmida, 8, Middlesbrough (from Libya)

:BE POSITIVE:

Be positive
Don't be angry
Don't hurt people's feelings
Be Kind
Make people happy
Make new friends
Don't fight with people
Don't steal
Be happy with everyone

- Sara Ahmida, 6, Middlesbrough (from Libya)

:THE WIND RUSTLES BY:

The wind rustles by
Flowers bend in its wake
The trees sway as the wind rustles by

The wind carries on its journey
As it's going to a very important place
Leaves sway side to side as the wind rustles by

It's halfway to its destination,
A very important place
For it is delivering a very special letter,
A birthday card is what the wind is carrying

Only a quarter of the way to go
It is getting dark
But it will not stop until it gets to its destination

It's keeping on going
And then it meets a sparrow, rustling its feathers
It is nearly at its destination
Come on, one more breeze!

Yes! It's there, it's at the birthday party
It drops the birthday card and helps blow out the candles
And then it's time to leave

- Alethea Archer, 7, Leigh-On-Sea

:THE SUN SHINES DOWN:

The sun shines down on the pavement
It bounces back up to the sun
When people walk by, their shadows shine bright

The sun lights the whole world from time to time
When it's done, we all go to bed
But some people are just getting up
As the world has turned around completely,
And the moon has come out

- Alethea Archer, 7, Leigh-On-Sea

:THE CAT, THE MOUSE, AND THE RAINBOW:

Rain is wet and splashy,
It goes drip drop as it falls from the sky,
It falls into a big puddle,
In the sky the grey clouds fly,

As a black cat creeps into the rain,
He felt wet and ran into the house,
He shook his fur and licked his paw,
Then went to chase a cheeky mouse,

The mouse ran away from the cat,
And went straight out the big, white door,
The cat ran out to catch the mouse,
But the grass was still wet, it soaked his paw,

Soon the sky was no longer grey,
The sun came out and the clouds turned white,
A rainbow arched over the land,
With each colour shining bright.

- Kaira B, 7, Berkshire

:SUMMER:

"It's summertime! The season to play in the meadows of flowers every day.
The bright sun shines on the picnic below, where your family and friends make memories.
Your adventures await on the beach, in the warmth, where your memories lay in the sand.
Explore under the water and waves and find glistening shells.
In summertime there's so many places to play and so many things to do.
I love summer!"

:THE RAINBOW:

"The rainbow has beautiful colours that shine so bright it tops the crescent moonlight.
When the sun is out and the clouds are sad, the rainbow appears to make them glad.
Everybody has a brilliant view of the rainbow and so will you."

- Sadie B, 9, Essex

:MISTLETOE IN TREE:

I spy,

      A green ball on brown bones,

      A pearl-strewn nest of emeralds,

      A wreath of green candles burning white flames;

I spy,

      An everlive crown for a skeleton tree,

      A halo for a saint of wood,

      An orb for a king of the forest;

I spy,

      A thief of energy,

      An advantage-taker on the disadvantaged,

      A parasite on an old life;

I spy,

      A tree-that-is-not-a-tree,

      A green-white charm of the mystic rite,

      A natural bough 'neath which to kiss;

Mistletoe in tree.

- Kit Bailey, 13, Derbyshire

:LISTEN:

Why do we harbour so much hate
Why can't we let it deflate

Is the world really that bad
That it can drive some people so mad

Can we not listen and let people glisten
Show them that some people really do listen

Trust me, listen
Some people believe life is a prison

Without a doubt, there is a vision
That will help you be driven.

- Jack Shelton Baker, 16, Sheffield

:AM I:

Am I invisible
Am I not

Can people see me
Can they not

Who am I
Am I me or am I not

Can I hear
Can I be heard

Do you know me
Do you not

Am I invisible
Am I not

- Jack Shelton Baker, 16, Sheffield

:THE ISLAND UNDERGROUND:

Sandown and Brading,
  Lake and Esplanade are fine,
there's Shanklin and St. John's Road,
  the first ends of the line
Ryde Pier Head's full of people,
  going on holiday,
and Smallbrook Junction's where you change,
  for the Isle of Wight Steam Railway
The old tube trains that work there,
  the 1938s,
along the line they trundle,
  going up and down and round and round
You're not a Londoner until you've ridden on...
  both the Undergrounds

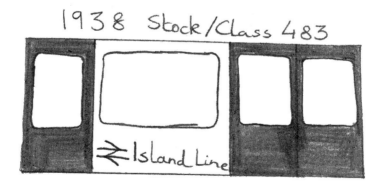

- Louis Baker, 11, Beckenham

:WHAT AM I?:

I have a tail,
I have 5 nails on my front paws, on my back paws 4,
I like to chase birds and squirrels,
I like to chase my tail!
I love to roll in the water,
I love to go for walks...

What am I?

Answer – Dog!

 - Alethea Bartlett-Rawlings, 5, Norfolk

:HEDGEHOGS!:

Spiky and prickly,
Squishy on their tummy,
They get really hungry in Autumn.
They get noisy, snuffly a bit squeaky before they get sleepy.

 - Aurelia Bartlett-Rawlings, 7, Norfolk

:WILDFLOWERS:

As pretty as a picture
So perfectly they grow
A summer breeze blows gently, so beautifully they sway
Oh I wish that I could join them
In performing their ballet
As elegant as a wildflower
Amongst fields of green
Freedom like no other
That's where I'd like to be

J D Batram, 16, Norfolk

:TOMMY:

Tommy was a Tommy
An English soldier true
He was fast and strong, a heart of glass and eyes the palest blue
Tommy was a young lad
From far away he came
With a boyish grin and unscarred skin, that wouldn't last a day
He marched and sang like any man
With his tin hat and gun, he was first to run
No time to fear machine gun fire
As he fights against barbed wire

Tommy was a Tommy
A boy aged 19, a husband, a brother and some mothers son
And in France he stayed
Buried in one mass grave
Marked with a white cross
Another life lost
In such an inhumane way

J D Batram, 16, Norfolk

OTTERS

Otters in the wild
To the water's edge
Two otters
Each otter into the water
Roam the waters
Sun setting

:POOS IN YOUR SHOES:

There is a poo in your shoe
Poos in your shoes
Poosiezoos
You're called loos
Cools!

- Prudie Beckett, 6, London

:SEASIDE:

Salt in the sea

Eels swim in the sea

A seagull swoops by

Sand on my toes

I love the sea

Dad gets me an ice cream

Eels on my hand

- Prudie Beckett, 6, London

:I WISH FOR A KINDER WORLD:

I wish I was a marvellous chef,
So I could cook all day long,
And make scrumptious, delicious dishes,
To share among the homeless whilst singing a merry song.

I wish I was an arborist,
Planting trees throughout the land,
To save all those poor rainforests,
Where the homes of innocent animals are nothing but sand.

I wish I was a peace ambassador,
To stop people from having destructive wars,
So we can live in peace and unity,
Come on let's welcome everyone with open doors!

I wish I was an eco warrior,
Fighting for our planet,
Global warming is destroying our Earth,
We have to do something about it.

I wish I could do many things,
But I can't do this alone,
We need to work together,
To save our lovely home.

- Neeva Bhudia, 10, London

:CABIN IN THE WOODS:

I want to escape to my cabin in the woods,
Surrounded by trees and dark shades of green
With my loyal companion bird or racoon or deer.
They don't judge,
They don't hurt.

I want to wear a white linen dress
And have my hair folded into braids.
I want to use candles when it is dark
And I want to sit in my world of peace
Which is filled with wistful music playing distantly.
I want to follow the sounds of that music
And see where it leads.
It would almost be like the music was glitter hanging in the air,
Waiting to be followed,
Like it is destined to be heard.
I would follow the sparkly music,
Running through the moss-covered trees,
In case I missed the song.
When I would arrive the person playing the music would be dressed
in a dark brown tweed suit
And he would finish playing the sparkly music and leave.
It would be my turn to play the sparkly music.
I would sit at a piano covered in vines and moss
And I would start playing my sparkly music.
Everytime I hit a key,
Glittery particles bouncing out of the strings on the piano.

Distantly I would hear fast footsteps rushing towards the glitter.
I would finish my sparkly song and get up from the piano,
I would say to the person standing behind me
"It's your turn now"
And then leave to go back to my cabin in the woods.

- Ava Bilinski-Smith, 14, Northumberland

:FROGS IN THE RAINFOREST:

In the Rainforest the frogs croak
When the frogs croak, the trees will grow
And that's for nature, nature and all.

- Samuel Bradley, 7, Cheshire

:THE WHISPERS IN THE GRASS:

The snow is in the mountains.
The grass is in the snow, when I'm snuggled up in bed I dream of the whispers of the wind.
When I wake in the morning the birds flutter and tweet.
The hot chocolate my mother makes smells delicious. I think I will have a sip.
When Monday goes I am sure to make yummy chocolate cupcakes.
The birds go south and the bears hibernate,
The mice gather corn and go off to store.
After winter Spring comes and the whispers disappear.

- Bethany Brand, 7, Suffolk

:CHOCOLATE:

Choose it right, choose it wrong, choose a

Hog, choose a dog, choose something cool, choose something

Odd. Choose a den, choose a log, choose a

Cat, choose a bog, choose something super

Off. Choose something... way...

Less! Choose something super

Amazing or something tall or something

Tiny. Choose something useful, choose something with

Endless uses or something not useful at all.

CHOOSE CHOCOLATE!

 - Benjamin Bridgwater, 11

:THE DOVE ("Fair White"):

The magical bird holds the earth,
With its big hands,
Flying, surrounded by stars,
Gleaming as white as snow,
In the deep blue sky.
Landing softly, its long hair,
Golden as the setting sun,
Cascades onto the forest floor,
She presented as a Maiden White,
Fooling all.

The handsome Prince she met,
Who fell for her illusion,
And wed Fair White that day,
But after nightfall, the spell was broken,
Fair White grew back her splendid feathers,
And flew off to the east.
The prince, heart filled with grief,
Angry as the red-hot sun,
Ran screaming, 'WHERE HAS MY PRINCESS GONE?'

He searched far and wide,
Through dangerous forests,
Over treacherous seas,
To the point of the North,
To the deep of the South.
To the West, then to the East.
He cried in despair,
Still, he did not find Fair White.
Wounded and tired, he headed for home,
Ready to live his life alone.

Back through the ominous forest,

The Prince's horse was alarmed,

A dove swooped down, startled the beast,

The poor prince fell to the ground.

He awoke to find the dove perched by his beating heart,

As feathers turned to golden locks,

He could scarcely believe his eyes.

His Princess looking down at him crying tears of joy.

Landing softly, in each other's arms, at last they'd ended their flight,

And here was their happy ending, he had found his Maiden, Fair White.

- Nerys Lilian Butler, 10, Ruislip

:SWIMMING:

The water is cold.
I shiver.
I dip one toe in.
And the water ripples.
I step in until the water is up to my waist.
It waves.
I glide in on my tummy.
And some of the water turns into little
Droplets that bounce of my face and slide into
the water.

But when I jump into the swimming pool.
The water reaches out of the pool and wets my face.
Or sometimes I fall into the water with a.........................

SPLASH

I swim back to the surface with water dripping
Out of my hair.

The water that was once cold
Is no longer cold
But is a pleasant warm.

- Amelie Callaghan-Till, 11, Downham Market

:WINTER TREE:

As my leaves slowly fall from my branches,
They touch the ground and whisper.
"As sure as night follows day,
Spring will come again.
The harsh winter months will soon pass over,
And a new flush of leaves will soon start to grow."

And that new flush of leaves,
Now not so very new,
They will start to whisper too.
"In the late summer months
You will drop us and then,
And then it will start all over again!"

- Charlotte Chillman, 10, Newark

:THE DAWN CHORUS:

Somewhere in the garden,
A blackbird trills,
A robin makes its call,
Perching on the birch tree,
They chatter and they screech.

Somewhere in the woods,
A crow caws from its nest,
A magpie hunts for shiny things to take back to its treasure chest,
Perching on the tallest pine,
They caw and twitter too.

Somewhere in Bilsthorpe,
A hollow old oak watches.
He says nothing,
But the wind whistling through his dying branches
Says everything for him.

He has seen many a dawn chorus,
And this one is as good as any.

- Charlotte Chillman, 10, Newark

:MY NEW BIKE (I LOVE IT LOTS):

I bought a new bike,
It is blue and red.
It has twenty two gears
So I can zoom ahead.

But I can't zoom ahead of my dad yet
Cos he's too fast for anyone.
He can do all the stunts,
But he also weighs a tonne!

It has massive wheels,
They are twenty four inches wide.
It has forks on the front wheel
To make it a comfier ride.

Also, you can stand up on the pedals,
And it has disc brakes.
It's called a CUBE bike
But it doesn't give you the shakes!

- Jesse Chillman, 6, Newark
(A tiny boy on a massive bike.)

:PINK:

There once was a dog called Pink
Who splashed in a puddle to drink
She jumped on a box
Got bit by a fox
So she ran and hid in a sink

:LEGOLAND:

Leaping with joy

Excitement across the park

Giggling children

Oh no!

Licence to drive

AAAAAAAAA!

Not that again!

Deep underwater creatures

- Penelope Chisholm, 8, Hertfordshire

:THE ANIMAL ALLITERATION ALPHABET:

Apes are applauding,
Bees are buzzing,
Cats are clawing,
      And
Dogs are dancing.

Elephants are erupting,
Fawns are frolicking,
Gazelles are galloping,
      And
Horses are hunting.

Iguanas are ignoring,
Jellyfish are jiggling,
Kangaroos are kicking,
      And
Llamas are laughing.

Monkeys are moaning,
Newts are nibbling,
Otters are observing,
      And
Parrots are pecking.

Quails are quacking,
Rabbits are running,
Snakes are slithering,
     And
Tarantulas are teasing.

Unicorns are uplifting,
Vultures are venturing,
Whales are watching,
     And
Xerus are exciting.

Yaks are yelling,
Zebras are zigzagging.
And that is the animal alphabet.

- Holly Christman, 8, Kent

:I HATE SPIDERS:

Spiders are scary.
They're ugly and they're hairy.
Eight legs go creeping,
At night when I'm sleeping

When I wake I see,
The spider staring at me.
I scream in terror and run,
And go and tell my mum.

She catches it gently,
And throws it outside.
I'm still so scared,
That I have to hide.

But every night I sleep,
Another creeps inside.
What are they doing?
Are they blind?

Get out of this room!
Its not yours, it's mine!
Leave me alone!
And then I'll be just fine!

- Imogen Christman, 5, Kent

:IN BED AT NIGHT:

In bed at night I taste pumpkins flowing through me,
In bed at night I taste chocolate,
In bed at night I taste honey and marshmallows,
In bed at night I taste sweet bats with honey in them.

In bed at night I feel the bones in me,
In bed at night I feel the blood moving around,
In bed at night I feel the door opening and closing,
In bed at night I feel the candy in me.

In bed at night I see the spooky pumpkins outside with spiders,
In bed at night I see spiders crawling around in my bed,
In bed at night I see the bats floating around,
In bed at night I see the spooky witches flying around eating
cauldrons.

- Rowan Clifford, 5, Flintshire

:IN BED AT NIGHT:

In bed at night I taste trick or treat sweets from the bowl,
In bed at night I taste yummy pumpkin pie,
In bed at night I taste juicy eyeballs,
In bed at night I taste my fear!

In bed at night I hear witches cackling,
In bed at night I hear bones rattling,
In bed at night I hear children saying 'trick or treat',
In bed at night I hear spiders crawling up my wall!

In bed at night I see cobwebs dancing in the light,
In bed at night I see Frankenstein walking around,
In bed at night I see scary witches soaring through the sky,
In bed at night I see something looking at me through my window!

In bed at night I smell candy wafting from the kitchen,
In bed at night I smell candles lighting up pumpkins,
In bed at night I smell a disgusting witches brew,
In bed at night I smell zombies rotting flesh walking to eat my brains!

In bed at night I feel scared,
In bed at night I feel like something is watching me,
In bed at night I feel something next to me,
In bed at night I feel there is something next to me!
Da, da, da, it is... an adorable plushy.

- Willow Clifford, 7, Flintshire

:AUTUMN:

Pumpkin picking, apple trees,
Misty mornings, chilly breeze.
Leaves rustle, squirrels scatter,
Woodland walks, owls chatter.
Hot chocolates and cosy jumpers,
Toffee apples and long slumbers.

I love Autumn.

- Lily Colarelli, 11, Bournemouth

:WINTER:

What a snowy season!

Ice is everywhere.

New Year is nearly here.

The temperature can be freezing.

Extra layers are worn.

Rolling in the snow can be fun.

 - Eva Crawley, 10, Preston

:WINTER:

Winter is the best season ever,
It's the season to be together.
Sledding, snowball fights until the day is done,
Oh My GOSH it's been so fun!
But now it's almost Christmas Day,
I do hope Father Christmas comes on his sleigh.
Mmm!!! Enjoying hot chocolate under the tree,
This has been the best for me.
Winter is the best season ever, it's the season to be together,
But now this poem is all done.
Bye everyone hope it's been fun!!!

- Isabelle Crawley, 10, Preston

:A DOG'S LIFE:

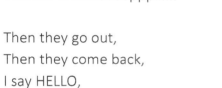

I say HELLO,
I cry for food,
I go for a walk,
I eat my food,
I have a bath,
Then....I SHLEEeeeeppp......

Then they go out,
Then they come back,
I say HELLO,
Then.......... I SHLEEeeeepppp.........

I defend the house from pigeons,
I go for a walk,
I come back,
Then........................
I SSHHLLLEEEEEeeeeeepppppp.........

 - Oscar Daly, 11, West Sussex

:UNTIL THE END OF THE LOLLIPOP:

The more you lick it, the more you lick it, the more you like it. The more you like it. The more you like it, the more you lick it.

- Piers Daly, 8, West Sussex

:MY FRIEND CHARLEY:

I have a friend called Charley
I dream of going to her house
We would watch her dog, Roxy
Who likes to jump, dance and bounce.

I have a friend called Charley
We would play Roblox and have so much fun
Eating pasta, chocolate and love hearts
Before we watch butterflies in the sun.

I have a friend called Charley
She is kind, caring and funny
I hope my dream come true so we can meet Maybe when mommy
gets some petrol money?

I have a friend called Charley ...
Everyone should have a friend like Charley!

- Isobella Davis-Healey, 8, Birmingham

:THAT IS WHY SHE IS MY BEST FRIEND:

I met my best friend, Edith, at school.
We were both four (but she is older)
She was always kind and helped me.
That is why she is my best friend.

Edith comes to my birthday parties,
we also have play dates.
She is so much fun and makes me happy.
That is why she is my best friend.

I like rabbits and Edith likes cats.
She has two kittens who are ADORABLE!
I was scared to meet them but Edith made me brave.
That is why she is my best friend.

Life is busy.

I do miss my best friend, Edith.

- Poppy Davis-Healey, 8, Birmingham

:PUCK'S ADVENTURES:

There once was a boy called Puck
Who fell in love with a duck.
They sailed the seas
their hearts full of glee
And the only way to go was up.

They saw a sail
They saw a ship
They left their boat
And hopped aboard the great big ship.
They heard a crying noise from down below where the cannons go,
And found that it was a curly haired black dog.
They named him Max!
They became Captain Puck and Duck Sparrow
And little Max...

Moments later Max found a treasure map!!!

The end... or is it?

- Ezra Demmer, 9, Norfolk

:WHAT'S A POEM?:

To be a poem
A poem has to rhyme?
No, to be a poem
A poem - well it just has to sound poetic!

- Aatya Rahardja Desai, 7, London

:AURORA:

A graceful dancer in the sky.
Her eyes shimmering like the Milky Way.
Her breath, the smell of raspberry ripple ice cream.
She dances lighting up the whole night sky.
Her perfect performance watched by everyone below.
Soft and silky she whirls across the sky with her colours swirling.
She sings a glowing melody,
"Now I have told you my secrets."

- Erin Douglas, 9

:THE OWL:

Screeching.
Flying, swooping.
Sharp talons, long wings, big eyes.
Spying everything on the ground below.
Perched high up out of sight.
Looking, ready.
Quiet.

:THE BLACK CAT:

Something is creeping in the night.
Eyes shining in the moonlight.
Claws out, ready to fight.
Tail slips away, out of sight.
A soft whisper saying "Goodnight."

- Erin Douglas, 9

:THE CAT:

Pink fur, pointy ears!
Green eyes shining in the night.
Her breath smells like fish.
Speeding like a ninja.
Soft and cuddly and cute.
A mouse friend on her back.
Sweet and quiet, she meows,
"Come here and stroke me!"

- Isla Douglas, 7

:OCTOPUS:

Octopus, that's me!

Crabs are my tasty snack.

Tentacles curling.

Orange, like fire.

Prowling for prey.

Under rocks, I hide.

Sea and sand for me!

- Isla Douglas, 7

:FIREWORKS:

Fun, fire, fizzle!

I see colours.

Red, blue, green and purple.

Everywhere in the sky.

Wizard lights then the magic starts.

Orange, gold and silver.

Remember, remember the fifth of November!

Kids are excited!

Scared pets are indoors.

- Isla Douglas, 7

:THE BULL:

I ate a bull which made me full.
But can I pull a bull???
I tried to pull the bull.
But all it did was roll.

:ME:

I wear crocs.
It's annoying when they say I have nice locks!
I gather sticks and rocks,
and i don't know if i've had chicken pox?

- Marco Drew, 9, Location
  Illustrations: Logan Drew, 11

:NINTENDO SWITCH:

The Nintendo switch, blue and red
It's so smart, it's like it has a head!
I play on it in bed
and in the shed.
The only problem is when the battery goes dead.

:BREAD:

Bread has no luck:
Bread is eaten by the ducks
It really sucks,
That bread costs 10 bucks.

- Marco Drew, 9, Location
   Illustrations: Logan Drew, 11

:MUSHROOM:

I once found a mushroom
the size of a balloon.
It was so big it looked like it was from a cartoon.
The top looks like the moon.
Hanging from it was a cocoon.

:THE CHARGER BROKE:

When the charger broke
It started to smoke.
I chucked it out of a window onto an old bloke.
Then the charger started to choke!
The charger broke.

- Marco Drew, 9, Location
  Illustrations: Logan Drew, 11

:FAMILY ACROSTIC POEM:

Family is lovely and kind. When you think about family you think stuff like love, caring, cuddles, kindness, pets, siblings, adventures, BBQs, Christmas, gatherings of course, ceremonies, yule and courageousness.

Also things like laughter, playing, forever, fun, helpful, team work, warmth and time outdoors.

My family have loads of memories like Camp Helions, my mum and dad's wedding, parties, BBQs, spending time together, Sonny, family.

I think of family as more than just a word. I think of it as my heart, my soul and I am always there for my family!

Lots of people can stop and say to a stranger "Oh yes, my family, I love them" But I think you should prove how much you love them by saying their names and this poem!

You always have family no matter what and they will always love you. I like to say "I love you to the moon and back" or "I love you always and forever". I appreciate my loved ones.

The end.

 - Alyssa-Mae Dutch, 11, Suffolk

:ROSES HAIKU:

Beautiful flowers
Leather leaves and soft petals
They have sharp thorned stems

Beautiful bouquets
Lovely fragrant perfumes
Delicate flowers

It is in my name
It is a summer flower
It's my fav flower.

- Saskia-Rose Dutch, 12, Suffolk

:HAYLEY IS A HELICOPTER:

Hayley is a helicopter
She can fly and glide
She can even turn into a car
Hayley is pretend.
The team will be there in the nick of time!
Shooting out water and steam and fire
And soap to make bubbles.
We fire her grappling hook
We get her hoses out.

RESCUE, PROTECT, SUPER HERO TEAM!
I am Spidey and can shoot out webs
Daddy is Spin and can turn invisible
Brianna is Poppygirl and shoots popcorn
Alyssa is Fizzygirl and shoots fizzy pop
Saskia is Little Lady and can throw water
Mummy is Supergirl and creates fire
Sonny was Rescue Dog but he died
Lily is now Rescue Dog but she is quite a bit rubbish,
But sometimes she's good.

Monster Trucky can drive super fast
So sometimes we fall over in him.
He can drive over mud and bumpy ground
because he has gripper wheels.
He can drive on water too.
Hayley can land on his back.

I like playing Hayley and Team with my family
Because I love my family and it's lots of fun.
I love my mummy and daddy so much
Because they play my games and read me bedtime stories.

- Tommy Dutch, 5, Suffolk

:THE SWING IN THE PARK:

I am a small, black swing in a park,
I never really get played with.
There's only one kid that likes to sit on me,
And sway on me, not swing,
I have a peculiar feeling that she also has got no friends of any sort. I don't know why,
But I feel like I've got a shy, quiet person turning into a friend,
Her,
And that she's got a new friend
Me,
I've never have had a friend as close as her,
Even if they are very secret to themselves,
But then, I am just a swing in a park,
And people think I've not got any feelings,
And not special feelings either,
But I do have as much feelings
And probably the same as that sad, strange little girl,
As a swing creaking and hanging off old, rusty chains.

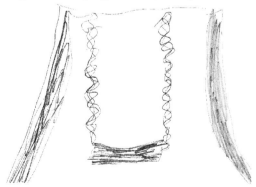

- Lilly Elwardany, 8, London

:FISHERMAN OR...:

I want to be a fisherman,
To me it sounds cool,
But an actor sounds cooler,
My friends say "No, you should study about Queen Victoria." But I
think I should be a fisherman,
"Why?" They ask,
I say "I don't want to study the past,
I want to be a fisherman."
And they say "Okay, we should listen."

- Lilly Elwardany, 8, London

:DOGS!:

Dogs, dogs, dogs, some have lots of fluff,
Some, like German Shepherds, can be very tough,
All dogs sometimes need a cuddle,
Sometimes they get themselves in muddles.

The Basset Hound has very floppy ears,
Their eyes look so sad, like they are about burst into tears,
They are short dogs coloured white, brown and black,
They like to sniff the ground to look for a snack.

The Husky has the work of pulling a sled,
They can sleep in the snow, but they also like a bed,
Huskies like to be in a pack,
They also like stuff to bark at.

Greyhounds are the fastest dogs in the world,
Their speed is a sight to behold,
They are bred to race,
But actually, they like a sofa and life at a steady pace.

The mighty Irish Wolfhound,
Is one of the biggest dogs around,
They are gentle giants that need lots of love,
They also need a very big rug!

The Pug has a wrinkly face and sometimes likes to take a nap,
Quite often on your lap,
They are also quite small,
And lovable.

The Chihuahua is the smallest dog and they like to play,
To make up for their small size, their bark often seems to say;
"Chihuahuas",
"Have got special pow-wowers".

The Corgi was the favourite dog of the Queen,
These dogs are bred to move cattle, despite not being very lean,
They have foxy ears and legs that are quite shorty,
And sometimes, like all dogs, they are a bit naughty.

The brown, black and beige coloured Labrador,
Likes to eat whatever they can get on their paws,
They can be trained to help the blind,
And are loving and kind.

The German Shepherds are very clever,
And are some of the best police and guard dogs ever,
They are coloured with patches of brown, grey and black,
Love for their family they do not lack.

The Dalmatian is covered in spots,
And when running they never like to stop,
They are white with spots of black or brown,
And as I have said before, they like to run around.

Some dogs are a mixture of breeds,
But loving homes they also need,
Some of them are goofy or scruffy,
Some of them like to play like puppies.

Some dogs become heroes who are amazing,
Togo was the leader of a team of huskies, though the snow they
were racing,
They were rushing to bring medicine to people in trouble,
Togo and his team did it on the double.

Laika was the first dog in space,
Who helped Russia in the space race,
Sadly, poor Laika died,
But she helped people understand space flight worldwide.

Bear was an Australian hound,
Who helped find animals in wildfires all around,
He wore little socks,
To protect his feet from hot sparks and rocks.

Dogs are kind and clever,
They will love you forever,
They are playful and happy,
And some of them are a bit yappy.

- Alfie Faulkner, 11, Farnborough

:KINGFISHER:

Kingfisher, kingfisher, by the quay,
Your feathers look like the bright blue sea,
Your chest, a rusty orange,
Your beak, a beautiful black tinge.

Kingfisher, kingfisher, by the quay,
Your sparkling eyes are looking at me,
Your amazing look of life,
Your wit as sharp as a knife.

Kingfisher, kingfisher, by the quay,
You perch up high in a tree,
Your shape so still and stiff,
Your head pointed down, like it will never lift.

Kingfisher, kingfisher, by the quay,
Your eyes spot in the water, a fish you see,
Your body looks like it is ready to dive,
You're now turning from still to live.

- Alfie Faulkner, 11, Farnborough

:A FOREST WALK:

This morning a noise I heard,
The sound was the song of a bird,
A round robin all plump and fat,
Was singing of this and that.

The woods were green and bright,
The trees made speckles of light,
The leaves crunched beneath my feet.
The smell of the trees was bitter and sweet.

I came to a stream bubbling and cackling,
Then I heard the sound of branches cracking,
A deer ran out of the woods and jumped the stream,
A lovely creature brown and lean.

A fish in the water gave a big swish,
That I could swim like that animal I wished,
The stones on the bottom of the stream glinted in the sun,
Each and every single one.

As I went on deeper into the woods,
I came into a clearing where a towering ash tree stood,
I climbed to the top, the branches were sound,
From the top of the tree I could see all around.

I looked down from the top of the tree,
And felt joy bubbling up inside me,
As I climbed down a branch at a time,
I felt a happy tingling down my spine.

Oh the forest makes you feel alive,
It makes your eyes open wide,
The power of trees and wood,
It makes you feel like you could do anything, go on I know you could.

- Alfie Faulkner, 11, Farnborough

:MY FAMILY:

My family is home,
Yearning for nothing more,
For love is what we have,
And we'll always be together,
My family is beautiful and loves beyond measure,
I am loved,
Loved interminably,
You have read our story, a love that lasts forever.

:HOME:

A home is normally a place of bricks and tiles.
But to me, it feels like miles upon miles,
Of happiness and smiles.
It surrounds you with love, which creates the roof, the doors,
The windows, the warmth.
A home isn't really a place,
It's a family, that holds you in its embrace.
Our home is the place of true love,
True devotion,
The place where true happiness lives.

Ember Fox, 5, Oxfordshire

:YEAT:

Yeat was a young warrior who carried a mighty sword,
His dark blue eyes were full of love and kindness.
He smelt of a wild Autumn evening,
As he moved through the forest,
Carrying his Sword of Truth.
"A warrior never loses his head,"
 He said in a quiet, husky voice.

- Luke Freemantle, 10, Ogbourne St George

:COBWEBS:

Cobwebs is green
Cobwebs is very mean
She flies on a broom
With her little black cat, Beans
Sometimes playing a tambourine
In one hand a Pumpkin Spiced Latte
In the other a giant big bag
Cobwebs is very mean
Cobwebs is green.

- Mya Freemantle, 13, Ogbourne St George

:THE SEA:

I remember the cold sea on my feet
The sky was so light blue
Where were the clouds?
It was very hot there
The pool was huge and nice
On a hot day

:PLANTS:
Plants dance in the rain
Plants are green
They give us life
Bees pollinate and butterflies too
The rain train goes around the world
The cold snow gives us a chill
The chill keeps us inside

- Chloe G, 8, London

:CHRISTMAS:

Crunching snow underfoot
Holly wreaths adorning doors
Reindeer bells jingling through the night
Icicles dancing from
Street lights
Twinkling in the night
Mothers hiding presents
And
Sisters finding them...

- Grace Gannon, 15, Teesside

:SADNESS:

Sadness makes you feel all tense inside.
Anger can strike too.
Darkness hugs tight when you are down.
Never a smile, always a frown.
Everlasting clouds above your head.
Sadness comes with a feeling of dread.
Soon the clouds will disappear, she said.

:HAPPINESS:

Happiness is the best feeling in the world!
Around friends is the place to be.
Performing and singing fills you with joy.
Playing, dancing and cuddling with toys.
In the garden joyful birds sing.
Near your family it feels safe.
Every day with a smile on your face.
Sat by the fire all fuzzy and warm.
Sipping hot chocolate, watching a storm.

- Isabelle Goldsmith, 10, Oxfordshire

:MY FAVOURITE TRAINS:

Steam Train
Big Old Smokey
Pulling Puffing Chuffing
Super strong, very fast, such fun
Scotsman

Steam Train
Big Old Smokey
Pulling Puffing Chuffing
So fast, streamlining, exciting
Mallard

- Oli M Grant-Barrett, 9, Gloucestershire

:UNTITLED:

Lions fight and Lions flee,
but all of them are friends with me,
and they are as yellow as can be,
if you ask me!

:UNTITLED:

Snow is snow,
snow is snow,
and incase you didn't know...
SNOW IS SNOW!

- May Hardy, 9, Edwinstowe

:THE DUCK POEM:

Duck was stuck under a truck while reading a book,
He was panic struck.
He wasn't having much luck,
So he took a look in another book,
And that book was on a hook,
And the book on a hook was a black book,
And that book was how to get unstuck from under the motor truck,
And the name of the truck was Nuck,
And Nuck was a pink truck,
There was a cheque book on top of a cookbook next to the duck,
On top of the cookbook was a sketchbook,
On another book was a pink book,
And he got unstuck from the truck,
Next to the truck was another truck.

 - Indie Hartland, 6, Guisborough

:AUTUMN TREES:

Autumn trees are pretty.
Autumn trees are cool.
They come in different sizes.
Medium, big and small.
I like autumn trees, do you?
With all their different coloured hues
Mustard Yellow, sap green and red
as I look through the window beside bed.
Bronze, indigo and violet too
Swaying in the wind as leaves do.
Lots and lots and lots of seeds
Producing fruit for our human needs
Sycamore seeds are my favourite of all.
They fly down from the trees that are tall.
They spin they twist they swirl from the sky.
Freed like a bird they start to fly.

- Sumah Hingah, 13, London

:A CAT WITHOUT A CHAIR:

A cat without a chair
Is like a rat without a hair.
It does exist, but it shouldn't.

:THERE ONCE WAS A MAN NAMED STEVE:

There once was a man named Steve
Who had a rhyming pet peeve
Steve's trying not to rhyme.
He's out of his mind
And now the cat's hanging from the ceiling

 - Aazer Hirst, 11, Grimsby

:MARIO ACROSTICS:

Mario is a plumber

And he steals Wario's coins.

Runs fast.

I like Mario.

On Yoshi he can jump higher

Luigi is Mario's brother.

Underground levels are medium difficulty.

In Super Mario Galaxy, Luigi can slide along the ground.

Gets a higher jump than Mario.

I like Luigi.

Bowser is an evil turtle with spikes...

On his shell.

When Bowser is defeated, Mario saves Princess Peach.

Son is Bowser Junior.

Every time Mario hits Bowser, the boss fight gets harder.

Really hard to get past him without a power-up.

Toad is a mushroom.

Oh no, the princess is in another castle!

Attacks enemies.

Dies if he gets hit and he doesn't have any power-ups.

Peach is a Princess.

Every time Mario defeats Bowser, she is saved.

A playable character in a few games.

Can float in Super Mario Bros 2

Has a pink dress.

- Musa Hirst, 5, Grimsby

:RESPIRATION ACROSTIC:

Respiration is breathing in air.

Epiglottis helps you not choke.

Some snakes can breathe through their skin if they're under sand.

Peacocks breathe through nostrils on their beak.

Intercostal muscles are my favourite part of the body – they

move your

Ribs to help fill up your lungs.

Automatic – you breathe in your sleep.

The trachea is the windpipe.

Inhalation/ exhalation – breathing in/out.

Over 21,000 breaths a day...

Now – take a deep breath!

- Salar Hirst, 7, Grimsby

:WINTER WALK:

Wrapped up in all my warm things,
Thick jumpers, a huge coat, massive boots,
Crunching through the soft looking white blanket
That covers the land as far as the eye can see.
Big steps making big prints.
Robins tweeting in the tall, imposing, leafless trees.
The usually familiar sights now strange shapes
Sticking up out of the snow,
Showing up against the snow.

- Shuky Hirst, 13, Grimsby

:I DON'T UNDERSTAND:

I don't understand a lot of things,
Like video games or social media.
But what I understand even less is the word ugly.
I think there is no such thing as ugly.
Why do people think dark skin is ugly?
It's not.
Why do people think afros are ugly?
They aren't.
Braces aren't ugly.
Spots aren't ugly.
Body hair isn't ugly.
You aren't ugly.
If anyone says otherwise, they're wrong.
And their behaviour is ugly.

- Shuky Hirst, 13, Grimsby

:THERE ONCE WAS A MAN CALLED DAN:

There, once was a man called Dan,
Who almost fell in a can.
He ran all day,
Lost his way
and fell into a pan.

- Yuunis Hirst, 9, Grimsby

.

:FAIRYLAND:

Dangling daisies, and flying figs,
Magic mountains and peppermint pigs.
Sparkly strawberries and wavy wands,
Candy glade gleaming, and goblin ponds.

Fluttering feathers, the sky glows pink,
White shiny wing tips, and cherry scented ink.
Laying on lavender, house walls are fluffy,
Roofs made of rhubarb, marshmallows are puffy.

Daytime is golden, nighttime is violet,
Candy-floss clouds and glittering twilight.
Rainfall of milkshake, snowflakes are ice-cream,
Lightning is sequins and swirling sunbeams.

Secretly saving, enchanted earrings,
Amazing melodies girls and boys sing.
Delicious dewdrops, tree trunks full of lemonade,
Chocolate never melts and smiles never fade.

Breadstick twigs, and branches of liquorice,
Lullaby birds, and invisible fish.
Oceans are custard, rivers are cream,
Throw in a stone to grant wishes and dreams.

Sugar leaves rustle, pastel-coloured fields,
Breeze of banana and rainbow-coloured shields.
Cupcake castles and fairy dust sand,
Such a magnificent place can only be FAIRYLAND!

- Harmonie-Rose Husk, 7, Essex

:SEASIDE STROLLS:

Seaside strolls and soothing waves lapping,
Turning tides making shifting sands.
Coastal creatures pinching and flapping,
Couples in love walk while holding hands.

Special messages swept out to sea,
To start their bottle adventure.
Shoreline covered in clumps of seaweed,
Sandcastles forgotten across the center.

Sparkling sea water hides sinking sand below,
Strong waves crashing cause collapsing cliffs,
Cool rippling surface hugs the suns' orange glow,
While providing the path for sailing ships.

Shiny, tiny shells on wind swept shores,
Saving stranded starfish as the tide changes course.
Excited, happy children ready to explore,
Not realising the danger of the ocean's force.

Bright, blue skies and ocean breeze,
Most mums hoping for a sunbathing session.
Turquoise swirls of the deep, blue seas,
Ready to teach innocent victims a lesson.

A blood-red sky arrives, sea silently disappears,
Sailing vessels drift out of sight.
No children running riot as the evening nears,
The lighthouse is a beacon of the night.

- Melodie-Eve Husk, 12, Essex

:PANDO:

Pando is my teddy bear,
He is the best.
Pando has his own chair,
If he needs a rest!

- Matthew Jackson, 6, Nottinghamshire

:BEE:

Hi my name is bee.
A honey bee I am.
Designed to make honey as in the name honey bee.
Just like me and you I have a specialty.
To make honey and buzz with my buddies.

:A LOVELY WINTER'S DAY:

Listen to the snow crunch on the ground
Freezing, frosty, frozen!

The sound of children sledging down the hill
Like rockets whizzing in space.

The feel of the nice warm fire
Dancing crackling flames.

The smell of hot chocolate
Milky, creamy and deliciously rich in my mouth.

The taste of Christmas dinner,
Succulent roast duck on a lovely winter's day.

-Kai Kellie, 9, Cheltenham

:LITTLE FLAME:
(In loving memory of the best rabbit to have ever lived, Margo.)

You were a flame, burning bright,
One day you blew into the night,
Every day you were dimmer,
You couldn't even eat your dinner,
So, so much chub,
I mean, seriously Bub,
Were you playing Chubby Bunnies?
Margo, it cost so much munnies!
I know you have no flame,
And there is no one to blame,
They thought it was a cyst.
Your spark blew in the mist,
You were put in permanent sleep,
With not even a peep,
You were only four,
You glowed so bright, but you were too sore,
But at least you did once glow,
Still ... Why did you go?

It's such a shame,
Life won't ever be the same,
You were epic,
Totally epic,
There's not a word for how I feel.

There is no bunny quite like you,
And you will live on in my heart for as long as I live,
And longer.

- Erin Kennedy, 9, Hampshire

:CYGNET:

There lived a cygnet.

That swam on a shimmering lake.

The cygnet was white as a pearl.

It glided, spying for tasty
food.

The calm cygnet found
A blue-as-sky dragonfly and
Gold-as-treasure wheat then

Gobbled it all up

SLURPING!

- Amelia Lakey, 10, Oxfordshire

:RAINDROPS:

Raindrops smell like
Blood-red poppies.

Raindrops taste like
Sour oranges falling from a tree.

Raindrops look like
Drips in the shower.

Raindrops sound like
Tennis balls
Boing, Boing, Boing.

Raindrops feel like
Sunset-pink candy floss.

I love to play with the
Raindrops.

- Ava Lakey, 8, Oxfordshire

:THE WATER DRAGON:

Me and my water dragon were looking at a big, long lake.
The excitement fizzed in my belly,
It was race day!!
My dragon was raring to go, I tried to keep her calm.
With a flash of lightening the race begins.
We dived into the lake, powering along.
The reeds touching us as we rushed past.
The finish is in sight!
I urged the dragon to go faster,
We swam over the finish line,
Happy and exhausted….
WE WON!!
I raised the trophy high in the air, I was proud of us.
We make a great team!

- Sophia Lane, 8, King's Lynn

:MY AUTUMN ACROSTIC POEM:

A season to be remembered while

Using the forces of nature to please us with

Tremendous beauty and

Unmistaken looks

Many of us dislike it but it will

Never stop nourishing us

- Finatine M, 10, Surrey

:BUZZ OH BRILLIANT BEES:

Bees bees they buzz in the breeze they buzz in the hot and they buzz in the cold so that honey can be sold in shops and stores and here we thought bees are bad oh no no no bees are buzzingly brilliant

- Hifzah Mahmood, 10, Birmingham

:THE RAINSTORM:

Once there was a rainstorm
It was loud and clear
The rain tumbled down
But have no fear
The plants and flowers drink the rain
They grow and bloom so right
Then we saw a rainbow that glowed so bright.

 - Rafaella Markham, 6, Essex

:EARTH:

Earth is an
Amazing planet, it has life and animals
Roar goes the lion
Tweet goes the bird, here on earth we are
Home!

 - Ruben Markham, 8, Essex

:MY CAT THEO:

I have a cat named Theo,
He was once called Cleo.
We didn't know he was actually a boy,
But it didn't matter because he brought us lots of joy.
Theo likes to run and play,
But sometimes he sleeps all day.
Theo is super smart,
And he has a big heart.

- Ibraheem Masoud, 9, Middlesbrough

:NEIL:

There once was a man from Deal,
Who had always wanted a pet seal,
He went to the zoo,
But got stuck in a queue,
And ended up with a narwal named Neil!

 - Eleanor McCann, 10, Southport

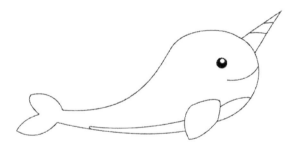

:FOUNTAINS ABBEY:

The fog weaved its way
through the cracks in the
cold stone walls. Mist, enveloped
the ancient ruins like a blanket.
Drops the size of bullets
hammered against openings where
stained glass windows once stood.
Falling like boulders from the universe beyond
the velvet black sky.

Fog cloaked the crumbling
towers like icing.
Stars glowed like torches
In the bleak mid-winter sky.
A breeze rushed in
a circle like a tornado
and the air was bitter and sour.

A monk silently padded along
the candlelit corridor.
Trees swayed and leaves twisted
making ghostly shadows
on the spiral staircase.
While the river
reflected the moonlit clouds
drifting in the ebony sky.

The low thud of the
monks' footsteps could be heard
on the cold, stone floor.
Their footsteps like the low beat
Of a military drum.
Suddenly, the chime of the solitary bell,
Echoed around the cloisters.
While thunder rumbled like an earthquake,
ominous.

A guillotine of lightning streaked across the universe.
As the chanting got louder,
through the storm the monks made their way
to midnight mass.
As their chants reached the altar,
A bolt of lightning lit up their way
Revealing gaunt faces and hollow eyes.
The faces of ghosts from long ago.

- William McCauley Tinniswood, 9, Greater London

:THE RED BLACK SOUL:

I used to breathe the sweet, damp smell of rain.
Oxygen now turned into fumes and fires.
The vision of seeing my home,
now destroyed,
haunts me hard in my heart.
The sun used to fill gaps through the leaves
in the looming trees.
Now the trees are gone and the sun
does not find a way through concrete.

Screeches of cars braking deafens me.
The warmth used to curl around me comfortably,
like a cosy hug.
Now, I am cold, bare, homeless and lonely,
my family all gone, long ago.
The winter snows were cold but I had a roof over my head,
my family around and food.
Now silence fills the gap where they used to be.

Gone now forever,

lost in their new surroundings.

All I have is the world around me and the long life ahead of me.

I am a lost soul in a lost body.

But once there was a fire inside of me,

a strength that I thought would never burn out.

But now I have

a lost bewildered heart in the forest of cities and towns.

For a brief moment, the fiery, crazy sun shone down on me

reminding me of the happy, sweet, joyful days.

Finding a small gap to pierce this new world.

I'd walk a million miles just for a glance of a home for me.

The lovely bushes and trees were a fox's playground.

A world cut down.

Now, bricks and rubbish heaps are my home.

- William McCauley Tinniswood, 9, Greater London

:A FIREY HEART:

His firey breath was
as hot as a burning coal furnace.
A rough, spikey tummy
With boil marks
And patchwork skin.

Wings that can hold a
hurricane. The spikes on his
back as twisting as a
staircase.
Twizzling round and round -
spiraling high into the clouds.

Claws like swords –
and as sharp as a needle.
With a tail which could slice an
Oak tree down the middle.

The dragon stands
tall and proud,
upright and straight.
Wrinkles run along his face like streams.

Blood red stained like
a streak through
his whole body.
Eyes shining as bright as the sun.
A shimmer in his eyes,
twinkles like the stars in the night sky.
He is a misunderstood creature.
A kind, intellectual heart
In a monstrous body.

- William McCauley Tinniswood, 9, Greater London

:RAINDROPS FALL:

The air we breathed was so sweet.
As moist as the steam
Which cloaked you like icing.

Echoes ran in circles
around the trees. Amidst
The lofty heights of my
Uppermost branches.

Dense vegetation builds the
journey up high.
When ripples
In the water stop the glass
Like still reflection.
Listen out for the calls;
squarks from spider monkeys
fill the Amazonian rainforest.
Layers of chirrups
from visiting birds.
Watch out for the
jaguar who weaves his way as
speedy as a bolt
of thrashing lightning.
Raindrops smash down on the hard,
Amazonian floor like bullets.

- William McCauley Tinniswood, 9, Greater London

:THE CONCRETESIDE:

The month is May.
A month of sun and melted concrete.
Too late for change
People didn't realise what
Would happen.

The trees were lost,
within the mountains of blocks
of grey concrete and red brick.
Like a game of hide and seek -
people ran to find one last survivor.

What was once a flowing river
Is now a streaming, roaring motorway.
Where old paths ran beside streams,
Lorries thunder past,
Shaking the ground to its core.
Animals hide, scared of the constant
Boom...boom...boom.

Towers keep us hidden
from the sun.
Locked and caged like wild animals used to be.
And never allowed to come out.

Shadows loom over the now
forgotten countryside.
Moments turning
Dark and sour as the world folds in on itself.

 - William McCauley Tinniswood, 9, Greater London

:TED:

There once was a monster called Ted
Who liked to hide under the bed.
He gives you a fright
In the dead of the night,
But he likes to eat jam on his bread!

- Albert Moore, 5, Whaley Bridge

:MEDUSA:

Don't be shy,
Just look in my eye.
Ignore the snakes,
Try my rock cakes.
Give a groan
As you turn to stone.
All gone?
Gorgon!

:SNAIL MAIL:

There once was a snail called Bob
Who really hated his job
He delivered the mail
Left his silvery trail
"I'm too slow!" he cried with a sob.

- Arthur Moore, 7, Whaley Bridge

:THE ARCHER'S LAMENT:

(On being ordered to execute unarmed French prisoners)
Agincourt, 25th October 1415

Muscles aching,
bowstring twitching,
Then stillness, pulse quickening,
my breath speeds up,
I see my brother's eyes in front of me,
Not my brother,
An enemy,
A prisoner,
A stranger,
He's standing before me, no weapon,
no protection,
Then I hear my mother's voice
'Don't do it darling,
what would your father say?'
His voice
One word
'Dishonourable'
Would they rather I didn't come home at all?
So I do it.
Guilt.
Shame.
Terror.
What have I done?
Where is our noble victory?

- Beatrice Moore, 12, Whaley Bridge

:UNICORN DREAM:

I watch as the hair sparkles and sways.

Hooves shimmer like glitter.

A horn that pulses as though it's alive

I climb up onto its back.

It walks, then trots, then it starts to run.

With the wind in my hair, excitement floods through me.
For even just that moment,
I feel like my whole world is happiness.

Beautiful shining magical
The horned creature starts to slow.
The unicorn stops, and I slide off.

"Thank you," I say.

Then suddenly, as clear as glass, I hear the unicorn

"Give me a name."

I search for a suitable answer.

"Luna," I say.

- Miranda Moore, 10, Whaley Bridge

:UNTITLED:

There once was a giant called Greg
Who had one very long leg
So he just hopped
Til his long leg got lopped
And his short leg became the long leg

- Miranda Moore, 10, Whaley Bridge

:NIGHT TIME HUNTER:

He pounces from fence to fence, sly
His bright eyes flashing in the moonless night
As soft as a teddy, he tiptoes by
His tiny prey will be in for a fright
The little legged creature scatters away
Disappointed, the hunter stares at the rising moon
Like a pale pond where ducklings stay
The twinkling constellations an amazing boon
Tired, he strolls to his bowl shaped comfort zone
Of course, the life he has is unknown.
That's the life of a cat.

- Ayah Mounssi, 8, West Yorkshire

:CARS:

Cars driving fast in water
It goes up in the air - sploosh!
And falls on the ground like rain.

 - Hussain Mounssi, 5, West Yorkshire

:FORZA:

I love gaming,
It's very soothing.
Racing incredibly immense,
It's a great experience.

Zipping down the track,
Never in the back
So fast I feel like my car is gonna burst,
But I handle overtaking the leader and crossing the line first!

So that's Forza for you,
The best racing game I know.
Just start your beastly engines,
Hit the accelerator :go, go, go!

 - Zak Mounssi, 10, West Yorkshire

:THE TITANIC:

The Titanic was huge

Interesting and beautiful

Travelling to America

An unsinkable ship

No!! Look out!!

Iceberg hit

Crashed to the bottom of the Atlantic

- Eliza Murgatroyd, 8, Gloucestershire

:LEARNING LATIN:

Lingua Latīna

Est lingua optima et

Eam nunc discō

Magistra mea mīr'est

Nos discāmus Latīnam

- Harrison Murgatroyd, 10, Gloucestershire

:BUTTERFLIES:

Butterflies fly,
With the trees,
And the flowers,
And the grass,
And the sun,
And the sky.

\- Darwin Overton, 5, Ipswich

:THE WIND:

The wind makes me feel free,
When the wind blows the trees whisper their secrets,
When the wind blows, I am bound to be climbing a tree.

- Seren Overton, 7, Ipswich

:UNTITLED:

Fish and chips for my tum, tum.
I love to eat it yum, yum.
When I go to the seashore,
I always want to eat more.

Then I go to play,
In the sunny day.
Penny machines to win a toy,
Makes me jump for joy.

Fish and chips for my tum, tum.
I love to eat it yum, yum.
When I head back to my room,
I dream about going real soon.

- Albert Palfrey, 6, Norfolk

:HALLOWEEN:

Halloween is a wonderful time! Yes, some may be
Afraid at the decorations and the costumes, but with this day there is
Laughing so hard that you feel like you're
Levitating, carving pumpkins while sharing spooky stories about
October, wondering if you should dress up as a ghost or a Werewolf.
Well, with this poem I invite you to enjoy this
Enchanted time of year, through the
Eerie music and the spooky night, and the
Noises that might give you a fright. This time is truly one of the best
                                                            times of the year.

- Tai Palmer, 11, North West England

:NOTHING:

No sound, or movement.
Offcut from everything.
Trees or skyscrapers? There are none.
Horrible, yet relaxing silence.
I stand alone.
Not a thing to be seen.
Good or bad? It could be either.

:AN ALIEN ADBUCTION:

All aboard the rocket ship
Loads of my green crew members pile into the flying saucer
I will now abduct some humans
Ecstatic with what we've beamed up
Now we will take them back.

- Aibhlinn Pearson, 9, London

:BREAD ON MY HEAD:

Bread on my head
Bread on my head
Save me from the bread on my head

Bread on my head
Bread on my head
Where is the butter?

- Ciara Pearson, 6, London

:CASSIE:

My dog's name is Cassie,
She's a fluffy spaniel mix.
She loves to chase the lead
When it swishes and it flicks.

She's got a lot of energy
And never does slow down.
And she's always super happy
And she never wears a frown.

Cassie will eat ANYTHING,
Anything she finds.
And as for tickling her tummy, well,
She never really minds.

She's one of us, a happy soul,
I hope it never ends,
Because Cassie and myself,
We are the very best of friends.

- Cordelia Pilmer, 6, Hampton, Middlesex

:WHEN I GROW UP:

When I grow up,
I'll be a policeman,
Perhaps a postman,
Or maybe a teacher?
A chef sounds nice,
But a doctor sounds better.

When I grow up,
I'll be a musician.
Perhaps a builder,
Or maybe a detective?
A journalist sounds nice,
But an astronaut sounds better.

When I grow up,
I'll have the best job of all!
Nothing's just right,
Except for
A kid.

- Laura Pinheiro Chaer, 9, London

:LOVING NATURE:

Loving nature all around you,
Loving nature here and there,
Loving nature everywhere!

- Elena Pinheiro Chaer, 6, London

:NIGHT SKY:

All is dark and quiet tonight
The sky is clear and looks like a sea of midnight blue
As I look up I see...
A kaleidoscope of magical colours
Bright pink is first and shines all around
With blues and greens coming to play
Blending high above my head
It's truly beautiful and mesmerising all at once
A shot of neon pink flashes like a lightning streak
Amazing sight to see
Aurora Borealis dances over the sky
They remind me...
How wonderful our world is
In what seems a moment they have gone
The Northern lights waving at me
Overhead outside my home.

- Lily-Mae Porteous

:THE TALE OF THE NIGHT:

On the night of November,
the air was crisp and the moon was full.

How it shone on the ripples in the water,
How it shone on the scales of the fish,
How it shone on the silver birch trees,

How the breeze shook the leaves,
How the animals came out to play,

and that my friends was the tale of the night

- Penhaligon Price-Davies, 8, London

:THE SEASONS:

Down in the meadows where the lambs are born
The bees are buzzing, and the flowers are blooming
Spring is here!
The sun is shining high in the sky and it's getting hot
It's the perfect time for the beach
Summer is here!
The weather is getting cooler, and the leaves are turning brown
Out comes the pumpkins and the treats!
Autumn is here!
The lakes are frozen and it's time for ice-skating and building
snowmen. At Christmas time we eat mince pies and drink hot
chocolate
Winter is here!
All the seasons are beautiful, and they bring us a lot of cheer, Spring,
summer, autumn and winter say hello until next year.

- Lisa-Marie Ramsey, 8, London

:HELP ME BLUME:

Colours, colours, colours; Red, green, purple, yellow and blue show your love and passion to Blume.
Colours, colours, colours.
Help me Blume.
Colours, colours, colours I love you.
Colours, colours, colours love me too.

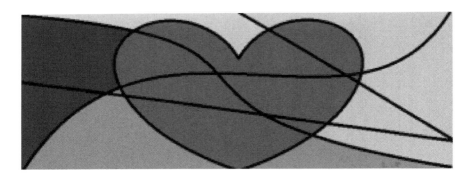

- Logan Rosa, 16, London

:ETHEIA:

Etheia, Etheia
Build me a house
Etheia, Etheia
Help me about
Etheia, Etheia
Don't be a clown
Etheia, Etheia
You're walking in town
Etheia, Etheia
You look like a fly
Etheia, Etheia
You're up in the sky

- Aletheia Xinyue Ruan, 6, London

:FOOD!:

I like food,
Yummy, yummy food
Pizza, apple, chips and fish
Sausages too, on a dish.

Fruit Shoots are a drink
Hot chocolate, milk and tea,
Coffee, coca cola and lemonade,
I wish they were all good for me.

- Persephone Xinxiao Ruan, 8, London

:MY BABY BROTHER:

My baby brother,
His name is Anas.
He's really very cute
And sometimes really naughty.
His cheeks are really squishy,
His tiny toesies, chubby
His teeth are sharp and bite me,
But his smile really lights me
He's nearly always cheeky
His laugh, a little bit sneaky
When I ask him for my pencil,
He almost hands it to me
But when I try to take it
He snatches it away.
He screams a noisy scream
And Daddy says to let him be.
He's always getting me in trouble
I used to be the youngest
But now Anas is that one
Even though sometimes it's hard,
Having him is a lot of fun.
I love him very dearly
He's the best baby I've ever seen
And I'm happy to be his big brother.

- Abdur Raheem Shaikh, 8, London

:TEDDY BEAR:

Teddy I always sleep with

Every day I put him somewhere safe

Don't know where he is sometimes

Down he falls from Anas' hands

Yes! At last I found him in the cupboard

Brown, and fluffy and oh, so cuddly

Each teddy I love, but Mr. Brown is my favorite

Always is there when I need him

Really he is my best friend

- Abdur Raheem Shaikh, 8, London

:FOUR O'CLOCK FRIDAY:

Four O'Clock Friday, freedom at last
Last week had not gone very fast.
On Monday, my school work, she asked for it quick
Oh no! I had forgotten, so then I felt sick.
Tuesday was just the same, my grades were so low
The other kids laughed at me for getting a zero.
On Wednesday, I lost my bag in the park
I looked and looked for it until it was dark
Thursday - well, you get the idea
Another bad day, I felt like saying, 'See, ya!'
Friday at last, I can be free
To play and relax – no misery!

- Muadh Shaikh, 10, London

:THE CAT:

A cat in the wild
hunts its prey
A cat at home
eats its prey
A cat in the wild
longs for love
A cat at home
needs no love
A cat in the wild
is soggy and wet
A cat at home
is nothing like that
A cat in the wild
has a tough life
Yet a cat at home
has no strife
Meow!

- Muadh Shaikh, 10, London

:FREE PALESTINE:

Over the years Palestine has shrunken,
Over the years Palestine has grieved
Under the oppression of the taker
You silently suffer
The world not knowing your pain
One day you will rise strong and reclaim.

:PROTEST:

Like a pot of boiling soup wants to escape,
Like a caged bird longs for freedom,
We want to speak out.
To ask for change
To make a change
To create hope and peace and freedom too
We ask for change in big numbers
Together we march and protest for what is right
To make a change
Is our right.

- Musa Shaikh, 12, London

:PRETTY KITTIES:

Cats are furry, cats are fun,
They play and nap in the sun.
Their purrs are like music, a lovely sound,
They chase their tails, spinning round and round.
When they meow, it's so sweet and nice,
Sometimes they even catch some mice!
They curl up in a fluffy ball, on the sofa, big or small, so cozy and
tight, dreaming of adventures all night.
They have jelly bean paws, and very sharp claws.
Their fur is soft like a puffy cloud and my cat Pumpkin makes me
proud. But sometimes she growls!

- Lujain 'Lulu' Shanib, 7, Eaglescliffe

:THE SCREAM:

I, pain, anger, and sadness. I feel them twist and turn and bend and merge caressing the blackness in my head.

Fly, scream, do what you must...   Silence.
Even though I scream for help, no one can hear.
Evil pain is crawling up on me. The pain of all the people around me
          zigzags in a labyrinth of angst and mystery
Laughing at you in the mist.

Pain is my drive. The sadness eats me away, the anger shoots venom
          into my fingers. The pain strikes at my brain making me
                    remember
And what I wish I could forget never ends. The sadness turns wild -a
          storm is brewing; an out of tune orchestra squeezes
                    out from
Inside. The petrifying blackness moves from my head to my chest.
          Eventually getting to my heart and pumping through my
                    veins.
Neel down before it. I feel it spreading and I scream because it
          hurts. Am I in Hell?

- William Simmonds, 13, Whitstable

:FORWARD:

I was running Forward
So close to the finish
I saw the billboard
I was soon to accomplish
and then I started slowing
My brother close behind
My muscles started failing
My brother was kind
We carried our way to the end

I did intend
to reach the end

:UNKNOWN:

Life on Mars, a world unknown,
   A barren land, with secrets shown.
    A quest to seek, a journey bold,
     To know the secrets, never told.
    A new frontier, a world to explore,
   To seek the answers, forever more.
    A challenge great, a goal to reach,
To know the worth of life on Mars, to teach.

- William Simmonds, 13, Whitstable

:ACROSS MY MIND:

I've been travelling up these mountains, to no avail, no white pig, no sacrifice to be held.
What can I do?
I travel another 3 mountains,
another 6 rivers,
Still no luck...
It comes across my mind,
what if I cover a black pig in white mud,
I continue with a new goal.
Another 3 mountains,
Another 6 Rivers.
I finally find a pig,
I cover it in white mud.
And I travel back 3 mountains,
I travel back 6 rivers...

- William Simmonds, 13, Whitstable

:GHOST:

People wonder why I'm the ghost behind the shadow
People wonder why I hide and run
People wonder why I make art

People hunt me down
People Hunt my art
People hunt my secret

I always want to help but won't
I always want to see daylight and dance
I always want to escape but Can't

Maybe I can stop
Maybe I can dance
Maybe I can show myself

- William Simmonds, 13, Whitstable

:THE TREASURE OF OLD:

Oldest story ever told
Events that will make your imagination spark
Where you'll hear the silvery song of a lark
Look for the wreaked ship
Last seen near the old tip
Follow not your sight but your hands
Harmony lies stuck in golden sands
The treasure she'll always hold
The treasure of old.

:THE GHOST SHIP:

The ghost ship that never sails
Always trying to rise but always fails
No one knows if it ever saw dock
Priceless cargo without a lock
The captain 'n' crew that should not be
Roaming the wild, dark and unforgiving sea
The ship that never sank
Held more than a bank
Search with all your might
You'll never find it with your sight
Look for the old tip.

- Taffie Smith, 15, Hornsea

:GLASTONBURY:

Glastonbury is my favourite place,
It is such a magickal space,
I really love it at Halloween,
When the Zombies can be seen.

We like to visit the mystical Tor,
From where you can see even more,
Of this special, beautiful town,
It turns my frown upside down.

It is known for its myths and tales,
Including King Arthur and Merlin trails,
Faeries, angels and witches galore,
This is why I want to visit it more.

- Joe Stanton, 10, Staffordshire

:SPRING IS....:

Everything's been hidden, behind the clouds, under the ground,
even the people who come outside.

The spring springs upon us.
Out spring the sun, up springs the flowers,
Here's the people.
Springing out the buildings.
The smells,
The flowers
The sunshine.
Birds singing on a spring morning.
I love the sun. It sets me free.
A spring in my step til the flowers rest
Blooming delight til I sleep at night.

The sun and flowers
Warmth on my skin,
Forage for plants.
I love to dance on the grass.
Flowers
Flowers
Pollen
Green leaves.

I was a seed falling now I'm tall and strong.
I am a tree.
Walking barefoot on the grass,
Feeling the earth of hints of warmth,
Life pushing through.

Hot dogs in the park on a sunny day.
Splashing in puddles,
wading through floods.
It's a different kind of niceness.

Springtime represents new beginnings and a time to start over.
Daylight.
Nature.

- Stoneygate Home Education Group (Collaborative Piece)

:BUTTERFLY:

Butterfly butterfly you fly high,
You make me cry when you fly by.
Butterfly butterfly you scared my cat,
She ran inside and sat on my hat.
Butterfly butterfly you flutter in Spring,
Your wings bling like the King's rings.

:GOODBYE SUMMER:

I will miss the owls hooting,
And the water guns shooting.
My favourite memory is boating,
I liked jumping in and floating.
I will miss my dazzling sunglasses,
As the hot summer passes.
I toss my summer hat,
And watch it land on my glittering bat.
I will miss sitting on my picnic mat ,
And gently stroking my milky cat.
Goodbye Summer.
Khadija Sultan age 6

 - Khadija Sultan, 6, High Wycombe

:INFAMOUS:

It's
Notorious,
Foul
And
Mischievous.
Our
Unhelpful
Satan!

- Henry Thomas, 9, Buckinghamshire

:BUBBLE OF FREEDOM:
(Sonnet #1)

My will is as the air, reborn and free,
Contained within a symmetrical sphere,
Floating above our wrongful laws to flee.
It's clear container glist'ning, nothing to fear.

When it was small and filled with helium
Untam'd and wild, ignoring "no"s and rules.
It grows; it's tasks increase. It steals and runs
Ignores and disobeys all taught in schools.

But when the bubble sinks all hope is gone.
The flashing lights lead me to disarray.
The cage of death, the bars of steel, none
Escapes. Everyone finds they're here to stay.

The open bubble bursts! Freedom is lost.
It stole and ran, free will the dreadful cost.

- Zac Thomas, 11, Buckinghamshire

:WHEN THE WIND BLOWS:

When the wind blows
On the windows
In the ocean breeze
Your worries go away
And when the wind stops
Rain comes down
The snakes go in their home
When the wind blows
Doors open and close
And when the sun comes out
People wake up
And then they draw love hearts in their books
And when the people go to bed
Always wish for dreams but please
Don't forget to marry the person you love

- Aizen Uchiha, 5, Leicestershire

:A GIRL AND A BOY LOST THEIR TOY:

Here's a girl, here's a boy
Up a tree
With their toy
Never knew
Never taught
How to walk
How to talk
Bring me up
Bring me down
In the air
on the ground
Rhyme up
rhyme down
Down to your toes
Down to the ground
Don't give up
Don't have a frown
Not good
Not bad
Truthfully said
Truly sad
Don't need that
I want my teddy back!
Don't cry
No need
I'm happy not sad
Because I have my teddy back!!

- Akemi Uchiha, 7, Leicestershire

:THE LIFE OF AUTUMN:

What I like about autumn is
That it looks pretty
And all the animals are out
Collecting food for when winter comes
You can decorate
In reds and oranges and yellows and more
It's a wonderful season
Drinking hot chocolate
Keeping cozy and warm.

Eva van Vuuren, 9, Norfolk

:PRISONER:

I live in a world full of pain and suffering
My world is as dark as a cave
The Master laughs at me every day like a menacing hyena

Inside I feel furious
I hope he chokes on his laughter
I feel determined to one day finally escape
His gold entwined in my hair
I will have my own shelter

But outside I want him to see a frightened, timid man
I want him to believe I will work for him forever
Roaming the fields like a caged animal
I want him to believe I will never escape

I hide dignity
I hide determination
I hide the passage to freedom entwined in my braids

To him it is my hair
To me it is my future

 - Bobby Wells, 11, London

:JUST A DREAM:

I close my eyes and I'm back there.
A collection of inescapable pictures
in the back of my head.
Almost forgotten - except not really.
Coming back to haunt me.

I'm trapped and scared;
Frozen in fear.
Tensed and terrified.
I can't help or move or stop it.
So, I stand defenceless
and I watch it as it happens.

It's like it's happening all over again.
A vivid reprise of things I wish to forget.
I want to cry, to kick, to scream
but my mouth runs dry
and no words come out.
So I watch it as it happens.

I shudder and its gone.
Like nothing happened-
I'm at home in bed.
Dripping in sweat, my pulse races
and my body shakes.
It's just a dream I tell myself.
Just a dream.

- Mia Whittle, 15, Saltburn-by-the-Sea

:NOT A SUMMER POEM:

Winter is my favourite season
It may be cold but I have my reason
It starts with a night of pumpkins and sweets
Of ghosts and ghouls, but also sweet treats

And then of course is the Christmas break
Christmas tree, Christmas crackers and Christmas cake
And some presents I hope if I've been good
And family and friends and Christmas pud

But my real love for winter comes in the new year
In the depths of winter before spring flowers appear
In the mountains of Austria, Switzerland or France
Where the landscape is white and the snowflakes dance

I like to ski but I love to snowboard
On-piste and off-piste, for that's what its called
I sometimes fall down but I don't care
Because the snow's soft and fluffy and lies everywhere

I speed down the mountain because that's who I am
Faster and faster, as fast as I can
Adrenaline rushing, the wind in my hair
An amazing feeling in the fresh mountain air

Even in summer I dream of the snow
Of sitting on a chairlift, the ground far below
On the hottest of days, my body craves cold
I dream of mountain adventures, yet to unfold

- Oscar Woolford, 11, London

:ALL ABOUT AMSTERDAM:

The tram was so bouncy,
I loved Amsterdam so much,
It's so lovely in Amsterdam,
The people there speak Dutch.

The flying seats were so long,
It was so funny,
I couldn't stop moving my feet,
The ride was very sunny.

The diamonds were so shiny,
I loved the laser place,
The jewellery was elegant,
I won the laser race.

- Clara-Elizabeth Worton, 5, Stockton-on-Tees

:AMSTERDAM:

The ferry was very wobbly,
The check in took an hour,
We went to the tram to our station,
My gummy worms were sour.

We went to This Is Holland,
The check in took 1 min,
We dove into the Earth rapidly,
The storm was a loud din.

The Science museum was massive,
I really love my Miffy,
The hotel door was cute and the room spotless,
The canals were straight and pretty.

We went to the Moco museum,
And saw some modern art,
We saw areas that looked infinite,
The inspiration came to my heart.

We went to the Eyefilm museum,
We got to Microtopia by tram,
Going back took seventeen hours,
I love Amsterdam.

- Finlay Worton, 7, Stockton-on-Tees

:THE DEEP DARK:

The deep dark is very dark,
You can mark an ancient city,
The warden is awful,
The deep dark is bore-full,
But the sculk is magically pretty.

:THE END:

The end is freaky,
Shulkers are creepy,
The enderman's black,
Chorus fruit is his snack,
The Ender dragon's mouth is beaky!

- Finlay Worton, 7, Stockton-on-Tees